Lunch Money

✳ And Other Poems About School ✳

written by **Carol Diggory Shields**
illustrated by **Paul Meisel**

PUFFIN BOOKS

For my mother, the teacher.
With special thanks to the talented teachers
and super students of Echo Valley School,
who brought these poems to life.
C.D.S.

For Donna, Amy, and Sara
P.M.

PUFFIN BOOKS
Published by the Penguin Group
Penguin Putnam Books for Young Readers.
345 Hudson Street. New York. New York 10014. U.S.A.
Penguin Books Ltd. 80 Strand. London WC2R ORL. England
Penguin Books Australia Ltd. Ringwood. Victoria. Australia
Penguin Books Canada Ltd. 10 Alcorn Avenue. Toronto. Ontario. Canada M4V 3B2
Penguin Books (N.Z.) Ltd. 182-190 Wairau Road. Auckland 10. New Zealand

Penguin Books Ltd. Registered Offices: Harmondsworth. Middlesex. England

First published in the United States of America by Dutton Children's Books.
a division of Penguin Books USA Inc., 1995
Published by Puffin Books. a member of Penguin Putnam Books for Young Readers. 1998

17 19 20 18 16

Text copyright © Carol Diggory Shields. 1995
Illustrations copyright © Paul Meisel. 1995
All rights reserved

THE LIBRARY OF CONGRESS HAS CATALOGED THE DUTTON EDITION AS FOLLOWS:
Shields. Carol Diggory.
Lunch money and other poems about school / written by Carol Diggory Shields:
illustrated by Paul Meisel.—1st ed. p. cm.
Summary: A collection of twenty-four humorous poems about school. including
such titles as "Math My Way." "Clock-watching." and "School Daze Rap."
ISBN 0-525-45345-8
1. Children's Poetry. American. 2. Schools—Juvenile poetry.
[1. Schools—Poetry. 2. Humorous poetry. 3. American poetry.]
I. Meisel. Paul. ill. II. Title.
PS3569.H48328L85 1995 811.54—dc20 95-7332 CIP AC

Puffin Books ISBN 0-14-055890-X

Designed by Amy Berniker

Printed in the United States of America

✳ Contents ✳

Eight-Oh-Three

Lunch box, backpack,
Papers flying free,
Shoelaces untied—
Eight-oh-three.

Quick kiss, oops missed,
Bam! Out the door.
Jumping, jamming down the stairs—
Eight-oh-four.

Legs pumping, heart thumping,
Running down the drive.
Will I make it, will I make it?
Eight-oh-five.

Tight corner, muddy puddle,
Dodge, jump, kick.
Slide into the bus stop—
Eight-oh-six.

Rumble-rumble, grumble-grumble,
Up the road it chugs,
Faster than a speeding snail,
Slower than a slug.

A moaning-groaning, blinking-winking
Yellow dinosaur
Slowly hisses to a stop,
Opens up the door.

I have a simple question,
I'd really like to know—
How come I have to run so fast
To catch a bus so slow?

STOP

Decisions

Menu, menu,
Under the magnet.
Buy my lunch at school
Or bag it?

Tacos?
Nachos?
Pizza with cheese?
Burgers and French fries?
School lunch, please!

Beef stew?
Baked beans?
Tuna-cabbage crunch?
Mushroom-chicken casserole?
I think I'll bring my lunch!

SCHOOL LUNCH MENU

Lunch Money

Don't ask Dad — he never has any.
Grandma's purse has a nickel and a penny,
Mom has a five, but the car needs gas.
Here's a dirty quarter someone found in the grass.
Checked all our pockets — nothing but gum.
Piggy bank, piggy bank, here I come!

Pledge

I pledge allegiance to the flag

Vanessa, stop pushing!

Hey, Joey, hey, Joey!

of the United States

I was here first.

of America

Whadya bring for lunch?

and to the republic

Ow, move back!

for which it

Sam, you're on my toe!

stands,

Eensy-weensy spider,
one nation under God,
Crawling up your neck!
indivisible,
Eeeeeeeek!
with liberty
No cutting!
and justice
No fair, Jeremy's cutting!
for all.

Code

I dibbin go to school today,
Bom looked at be and said, "No way."
Wend back to bed and here I'll stay,
'Cause I hab a terrible code.

By throad is sore, by eyes are bink,
By node dribs like a leaky sink,
By head's so stuffed it hurds to think.
I hab a terrible code.

And the Answer Is...?

Teacher, please don't look at me —
The answer is a mystery.
I'm staring into empty air,
I'm sliding underneath my chair.
I'm making myself very small,
I wish I wasn't here at all.
Teacher, teacher, pass me by,
Please pick on some other guy.

Teacher, teacher, call on me —
I know the answer, can't you see?
This one's a wrap, a snap, a breeze.
Just look in my direction, please!
I'm almost bouncing off my chair,
I'm waving both hands in the air.
Teacher, teacher, ask me first,
'Cause if you don't I think I'll burst.

Math My Way

Two plus two is twenty-two.
It's plain as day that this is true.
But teacher says she's very sure
That two plus two adds up to four.

Three plus three makes thirty-three.
That's the way it ought to be.
But teacher says the answer's six.
I don't know why. Must be a trick.

Four plus four is forty-four.
Not any less, not any more.
My teacher just can't get it straight.
She keeps on saying the answer's eight.

I give up. I'll go along.
I'll do it her way, though she's wrong.
But in my heart, I know what's true—
Two plus two makes twenty-two.

Amanda

I think Amanda likes me.
I think Amanda cares.
Today she kicked my lunch box
Halfway down the stairs.

I think Amanda likes me.
I think it's really true.
At the hallway fountain,
She spit water on my shoe.

I think Amanda likes me.
I knew it when she said
She thinks I'm gross, disgusting,
And a total cootie-head.

Simon Says

Simon says Sarah says Evan told Jamie
That Megan told Morgan that Mandy told Amy
That Kelsey told Casey, and Casey told Ryan,
And Ryan told Chuckie, and Chuckie told Brian,
And Brian says Holly says Molly says Polly says
Hannah says Anna says she'll never tell.

School Daze Rap

Woke up at eight—oh no, I overslept!
I ran for the bus, but the bus had left.
I raced to school, I really, really buzzed,
But then I forgot where my classroom was.
Finally found it, opened the door—
My teacher turned into a dinosaur!
The dinosaur roared, "Sit down at your desk!
Pick up your pencil, 'cause we're having a test!"
All the kids were staring, sitting in their rows,
I looked down and saw I'd forgotten my clothes.
The dinosaur frowned and started to shake me,
Turned into my mom, who was trying to wake me.
"Hey, sleepyhead, Tommy's here to play,
Why aren't you up? It's Saturday."

Rosie

Have you met our Rosie yet?
She's very, very sweet.
We love her from her round pink ears
Down to her tiny feet.
Be gentle, you can take her out—
She'll climb up on your shoulder,
And even Jake sits quiet when
He gets a turn to hold her.

Her whiskers are all twitchery
Around her pretty nose,
And it really, really tickles
When she crawls inside your clothes.
We like to share our snacks with her
(She's getting kind of fat).
She's everybody's special friend—
She's Rosie, our class rat.

Eddie Edwards

Eddie Edwards runs around.
He never shuts up, he never sits down.
He teases the girls, he cuts in line,
He never makes it to school on time.

Eddie Edwards does sound effects,
Like sirens and lasers and racing-car wrecks.
His pen has a leak, his binder's a mess,
And you wouldn't believe what he keeps in his desk.

Eddie Edwards' socks don't match.
His hair looks like a blackberry patch.
His shoelaces dangle like dirty spaghetti,
And I wish that I could be just like Eddie.

Who Needs School?

Read it? Forget it — I'll get the video.
My calculator takes care of my math.
Don't need art, my computer has graphics,
This spell-checking program makes spelling a laugh.
No need to write, since I got a printer,
And my preprogrammed keyboard plays music divine.
I don't need friends, 'cause I have Nintendo.
Just don't unplug me and I'll be fine.

Recess Rules

No sliding down the handrails.
No climbing up the slide.
No bouncing on the seesaw.
No throwing sand outside.
No twisting on the swings.
No climbing up the trees.
No jumping from the fences.
No hanging by your knees.

Max slides down the handrails.
He climbs right up the slide.
Max bounces on the seesaw.
He throws the sand outside.
Max twirls the swings up double.
He calls me from a tree.
I climb up. Who gets in trouble?
Max sure doesn't.
Only me.

23

Swap

Mom made me a peanut butter sandwich,
I traded at lunch for a tuna on rye.
Swapped my orange for Jonathan's corn chips,
And traded my cookies for a marshmallow pie.

Traded the chips for a handful of pretzels,
Gave up my milk for a tropical punch.
Changed the tuna for Ben's bologna,
Swapped the pie for the cake in Kim's lunch.

Gave the bologna for a bagel with cream cheese,
Swapped the cake for yummy Gummy Bears.
Sold the punch for a shiny, new quarter,
Traded the pretzels for a nice, ripe pear.

Bought some cold milk with the quarter,
Traded the bears for a pudding cup.
Swapped the bagel for Joe's ham sandwich,
Exchanged the pudding for a Fruit Roll-Up.

Gave the ham for a peanut butter sandwich,
Took an orange for the fruit roll snack.
Swapped the pear for two chocolate-chip cookies...
I think I just got my old lunch back.

Outside / Inside

Outside, the sky is cracking,

The leaves are snapping,

The flag is slapping.

Inside, we are coloring maps.

Outside, the wires are strumming,

The air is humming,

A storm is coming.

Inside, we are doing the states.

Outside, I would shout into the wind,

I would twirl, dance, and spin,

Feel the rain against my skin.

Inside, I am making Michigan blue.

27

The Big, Bad Wolf

The big, bad wolf was picking his nose,
The little pig's tail fell down.
Rumpelstiltskin forgot his name,
Cinderella tripped on her gown.

Goldilocks knocked — the door fell in,
Papa Bear started to cry.
Rapunzel punched Pinocchio,
The blackbirds got stuck in the pie.

Little Red Riding Hood sat on Miss Muffet,
Two billy goats ran the wrong way.
It was a great show. We all shouted, "Bravo!"
For the kindergartners' play!

Whew!

I didn't get my spelling done,
My science was a mess,
I totally forgot about
The social-studies test.

Finished only half the math,
My essay was too short,
The baby finger-painted jam
All over my report.

On the bus, I lost my pen,
And when I got in line,
I couldn't find the papers
My parents had to sign.

I gave up hope, went into class,
Shaking in my boots,
And saw the greatest sight on Earth—
A smiling substitute.

Far Away

Someone shouts in Annie's ear,
But what they're saying, she can't hear.
Buzzers buzz and school bells ring,
Annie doesn't hear a thing.
Friends can jostle, tug, and pinch,
Annie doesn't move an inch.
"Oooo, here comes a big black bug!"
Annie does not even shrug.
"Fire!" "Earthquake!" "Runaway bus!"
She remains oblivious
Until, at last, with a faraway look,
Annie smiles and shuts her book.

Spinning Song

We're spinning,
  we're spinning,
    we're spinning
     around,
    Downside
      up and
       upside
        down.
We're whirling,
  we're twirling,
    we're head
     over heels,
Pinwheels and
    spinwheels,
     and Ferris
      wheels.

Whirl-i-gigs,
girl-i-gigs,
spinning
in place,
Spinning
in time,
spinning
in space,
Spinning
right off
of these
monkey bars,
Spinning
like planets
around
the stars.

Clock-watching

The big hand jumps, two minutes at a time,
   Click, jump. Click, jump.
      Counting out the minutes till we get in line,
       Click, jump. Click, jump.
         Counting out the minutes till school is done,
          Click, jump. Click, jump.
          Counting out the minutes
             till we have some fun.
        Click, jump. Click, jump.
       I'm wiggling, jiggling, tapping my shoe,
      Click, jump. Click, jump.
     Thinking of things I'm going to do.
    Click, jump. Click, jump.

Call a friend, maybe ride my bike,
Read a book, do whatever I like.
Play some games or just relax,
Fix myself a few good snacks.
Mess around, ignore my chores,
Maybe just lie in the sun outdoors.

Watching that clock moving slow as glue.
Click, jump. Click, jump.
Funny, but my students are watching it, too.

Moonwalker

I'm a moonwalker, walking on the moon.
I'm a jungle stalker, stalking wild baboons.
I'm a superhero, skimming through the blue.
Puddle jumping, leaf-pile leaping, I'm a kangaroo.

I'm a desert rattlesnake, sliding through the sand.
Counting out the beat, I'm the leader of the band.
I'm Tyrannosaurus, looking for a snack.
Whoo-whoo! I'm a train, rolling down the track.

I'm a red-eyed robot, clanking up the road.
I'm an eighteen-wheeler with a heavy load.
I'm a famous rock star, moving very cool.
Actually,
        I'm just me,
                Walking home from school.

I'm Doing My Homework

I'm doing my homework,
And I have found
If I bite my pencil all around,
It makes an interesting pattern of holes
That help my pencil not to roll.

I'm doing my homework,
And I've discovered
If I cross my eyes at my math-book cover,
The letters all smush and kind of float,
And it looks like something a Martian wrote.

I'm doing my homework,
And I have found
I can make a lot of different sounds
By hitting my pen on the side of my bed
Or my teeth or my chair or the top of my head.

I'm doing my homework.
Some kids think it's dumb,
But I think homework is kind of fun.
The assignments are sometimes boring, it's true,
But somehow I always learn something new.

Book Report

This was a very, very, very nice book.
The story was very, very, very, very good.

16 words.

You would like it very, very much
If you read it, and I think you should.

32 words.

The plot was very, very interesting,
About some kids who were very good friends.

Finally got to 50 words,
If you count...

THE VERY, VERY END